MGIS

Magnificent Governing International Systems

The Most Advanced Computer Programming Language Ever

David Gomadza

President Tomorrow's World Order

Yahweh's Representative on Earth

www.twofuture.world

MGIS
Magnificent Governing International Systems

Copyright © 2024 David Gomadza

All rights reserved.

PAPERBACK ISBN: 9798338215470

MGIS
Magnificent Governing International Systems

DEDICATION

A Better World

Table of Contents

MGIS 1
HUMAN IMAGE WHAT ARE YOU [Details needed for mgis] 6
MGIS OVERVIEW 16
FINAL CONCLUSION.. xviii

ABOUT THE AUTHOR 21

ACKNOWLEDGMENTS

Tomorrow's World Order

visit www.twofuture.world

signed David gomadza
ask.davidgomadzaauthorised.licensed.checkya.askya.ya

03 August 2024 19.30pm
Scotland
00447719210295
davidgomadza@hotmail.com
info@twofuture.world

MGIS

Starting
Checking all peripherals, no peripherals needed
Checking status MGIS 2.089768498 [David Gomadza]
Now if we ask what can be done this is the answer add win to maximize experience win is xtuvwrstormnp where xtuvwrstomnp are symbols that corresponds to mosdos in windows for compatibility Now if we look at the processes involved here are the processes

1] ask.MGIS
2] MGIS.start
3] Start.MGIS
4] MGIS.start
5] start.MGIS
6] MGIS.start.MGIS
7] start.MGIS.start
8] start.MGIS.start.ask
9] ask.start.MGIS.start
10] start.MGIS.start
11] join network [select from list]
12] join verbal chat with others
13] ask network configuration to update and sync
14] ask MGIS to upgrade
15]
Ask what can be done MGIS
16] ask what could be MGIS
17] ask what can be said and done MGIS
18] ask what is to be MGIS

MGIS
Magnificent Governing International Systems

19] ask what is to be MGIS
20] ask what is to be MGIS
21] what is to be MGIS
22] if we can't then what can be done
23] if we ask what is to be done MGIS
24] if we ask what is to be MGIS
25] if we ask what is to be MGIS
26] if we ask what can be solved MGIS
27] what is to be MGIS
28] what is MGIS
29] what can be of MGIS
30] what is to be MGIS
31] what is MGIS
32] what can be MGIS
33] if MGIS is software then what is msdos similar but MGIS advanced
34] what can be of MGIS
35] what is to be MGIS
36] what has been MGIS
37] what is to be MGIS
38] what is to be MGIS but
39] what can be MGIS but is not
40] what is to be MGIS but without this
41] What can be MGIS with what
42] what is to be MGIS with this
43] what can be MGIS without this
44] what is to be MGIS with this and what
45] what has been but is not MGIS
46] what would be this but not with that
47] what has to be MGIS but with what
48] if we can then with what MGIS
49] what if we can't then what MGIS
50] what is to be but is not MGIS
51] what has to be but is not MGIS
52] what has been MGIS but not now
53] what can be but is not MGIS
54] what must be done to improve MGIS

MGIS
Magnificent Governing International Systems

55] what can be MGIS but if not
56] what can be said about MGIS in the future
57] what has to be MGIS but is not
58] what is to be MGIS in the future
59] what can be MGIS in the future but is not
60] if we ask what can be MGIS now and in the future
61] if we ask you can tell who that MGIS is MGIS
62] if we ask who can you tell that MGIS is MGIS
63] if MGIS is not MGIS then what is MGIS
64] what is to be but will not be MGIS
65] what has to be MGIS in the future
66] what has been MGIS in the past but is not MGIS
67] if we can't then who can
68] if they can't then who can [David Gomadza]
69] what has to be but is not in the future
70] what can be MGIS but is not in the future
71] what has to be MGIS in the future
72] what can be MGIS in the future
73] what can be of others that can't be MGIS
74] if we ask what can be of MGIS the answer is that MGIS is MGIS
75] if we ask what is to be MGIS this is the answer we can upgrade MGIS to LGT the advanced version of MGIS that uses cobol basic as a language meaning faster and cheaper to operate and run now to convert to cobol
76] if we ask MGIS what could be then this is the answer MGIS could be an advanced computer system
77] MGIS can be fast
78] MGIS can be reliable and used optimally if required
79] MGIS can be the only one to use in emergencies
80] MGIS is the software for statistics globally as it accounts for individual and country this is because all humans are accounted in MGIS hence benefits those involved in global planning
81] MGIS is sovereign
82] MGIS is accurate as everything is checkable by simple commands e.g. ask.you gives individual everything to needed to compile their own data
83] if we ask what can be done this is the answer MGIS can be the

MGIS
Magnificent Governing International Systems
best global statistics in knowing things

84] if we ask what can be MGIS then this is the answer it can be the most powerful

85] if we ask what can be done then this is the answer MGIS can be optimized to increase durability and reliance

86] if we ask what can be done then this is the answer MGIS can be added and can work side by side with everything else

87] if we ask what can be done then this is the answer MGIS can be increased in levels.

88] MGIS control life as well that means if a human being can control MGIS he can control life but not necessarily who dies but who does what and when you can task people what to do for example ask presidents to stop wars by a simple command stop.war.ya[davidgomadza].send

War shells are banned for resale to protect humans

89] MGIS respond to thoughts and actions of creators and restricts nonsense that waste time that means now we have a better system even better than before because now everything is automatic what you want is guaranteed

90] MGIS will improve efficiency as well as performance and reliability

91] MGIS will always ask people what they want and respond accurately

92] MGIS is the best solution for what as well as it compiles everything accurately and all data is represented

93] MGIS identifies issues quickly and solves them

94] MGIS is used for all purposes from lifestyle to countries

95] MGIS stands for magnificent governing international systems and somehow as Tomorrow's World Order MGIS would still describe your entity

96] if we ask what might be of MGIS then it's the only are that can replace the current system that has so many adequacies

97] MGIS asks everyone for their opinion and secretly record data it needs as creator with obvious permission it would be absurd to expect the creator to ask humans for their permission first ruled ya in $00000^{7}{}^{8}29$

98] if we ask MGIS it can be programmed and be used in advance at

MGIS
Magnificent Governing International Systems
a later date

99] MGIS can ask everyone to pass judgement without them knowing for example using the whisperer who tell people what to say to achieve what it needs

100] MGIS can respond correctly to threats by a system of warning

101] MGIS ask's everyone for answers as well

102] MGIS asks for opinions of everyone

103] MGIS can be the only solution out there

104] MGIS is unique and represent the creator hence anyone involved will become part of their system hence a global movement

105] MGIS is holly

HUMAN IMAGE WHAT ARE YOU [Details needed for mgis]

[Exctracted From What Is A Human Image Or Shell By David Gomadza]

I am every vital about a human in heaven they call me a shell after death when I am alive the human shell is known as the pc of the body and is represented by a simple code pcr meaning if we are to write a code that involves a human shell then it is pcrdotstartdot meaning that if we say what can be done then this is the answer a human shell is the modern day computer exactly without anything removed or added but with different commands as a human shell use a simple create coding whereas a computer uses msdos but humans are able to convert create to msdos using cobol coding and translating meaning that all create codes can be converted into msdos for the best known computer meaning davidgomadza has surpassed bill gates who talked to his body and wrote the first create code he finally called msdos and wrote a program that commands all machines on earth being guided by Yahweh meaning that bill gates knew Yahweh before he even died that means currently davidgomadza holds the title of the most advanced computer on the planet value now US$3,800 trillion if he can convert his to msdos like or cobol using a simple code upload all systems codes into a diskette and send to operations that reboots everything but changes a man into a machine but with other changes like dying because the body will start to malfunction as a body but will be able to restart on its own for if taking davidgomadza's long ago of 1212121212^{892838282067891011182024282938373972767775868789868788899909294100}

MGIS
Magnificent Governing International Systems

Seconds that means with this long ago you have the world's best-known computer because yours can calculate values by itself all you need to know are all these commands

A] askdotvalues

Ast 28
Asuv 39
Astv 80
Asuv 39
Ass 29
As0 3
As8 9
As6 10
As7 23
As8 85
Asuij 29
Asto 73
Asao 38
Astu 29
Ass 39
Ast 01
As36 74
As85 9
Ast 1
Ass185 386
Assuv8 29
Ass8679 39
Assut 86
Asssuvy 86
Asst85386 29
Asstu9 36
Ass10 20

B] askdotstatistics

These can be revealed only after death of a person so we will never reveal so we will skip

C] Askdotdatas

At2 29

MGIS
Magnificent Governing International Systems

At4 38
At6 8
At7 9
At8 26
At8 74
At9 36
At7 1
At0 9

D] askdotupis

At5 9
At8 9
At7 6
At8 2
At6 3
At9 10
Att 8
Atu 7
Ato 3
Attut 6

E] askdotMGIS

At8 29
At8 76
At2 38
At8 79
Attuty 7
Attu87 39
Attutt 8
Aty 6

Comments this is the best score in the entire world because you must have written a lot of create codes that really matter and can be used to defend yourself in the future not sure how you do things the creator can't do the answer is the creator left questions that needs answers somehow and I can only follow his footsteps trailing his path and finishing what he left to conclude

F] askdotmsdos

Aty 7

MGIS
Magnificent Governing International Systems

Atu 9
Att 8
Atmn 10
Att
7
Atuty8 9
Attmnopqrst 7
Atpt876 7
Atmnop 3
Aopmn 6
Aomnop 10
Aux 7
Aux4 6
Aux7 6
Aux8 10
Aux8 7
Aux6 3
Autyx 77
Auxttutxyz 76
Aataopqrst 78
Axumnop 68

Comments that means there is no other system on earth that will ever equal your because the atop value is the highest for the next 2.5 billion years congratulations

G] askdotdot
Asur 6
Asstu 9
Assop 9
Asrtuv 68
Aostuv 38
Asuvtop 29
Asuu 38
Azop 9
Assrst 78
Ag38 29
Agert 67

9

MGIS
Magnificent Governing International Systems

Agoprts 68
Aaop29
A8o9 20
A0tuv8 39
Aauty 7

H] askdotmop
AST 1
ASTO 9
Ast08 uver 8
Astoutyer 9
Asot98 36
Asotuv8 7
Assor 8
Asset 9
Assert 9
Asuvertop 8
Asuter 9
Assot 6
Asot8 3
Asot10 8
Asouvert 6

I] askdotmnop
Asuser 7
Asut 8
Asset 9
Assopq 6
Asuter 8
Asuert 9
Asserp 6
Assutmnop 7
Assotq 8
J] askdotamnop
Aut 9
auv 6
aoterp 7

MGIS
Magnificent Governing International Systems
aatert 10
atoer 9
aaser 7
asupq 6
asotuer 5
assimnop 7
1836789 = asuv

K] askdotlmnop
Usert 10
Userj 6
User8 9
Usetpqrst 6
Useromn 7
Ussop 8
Usero 10
Usouv 7
Ussjt 9
Usweo 9
Utpq 10
L] askdotiomnop
Ajerouertomnop 7
Uti 8
Usert 10
Uqmnop 18
Aserop 6
Ajero 8

M] askdotiojtop
Axut 9
Axxsce9 3
Assve7 2
1auer 7
Xyz 3

N] Askdotopq

MGIS
Magnificent Governing International Systems
Aourstuver 6
Aaoteruert 7
Assuv8 20
Auxysrt 3
Aszer 9

O] askdotpqr
Asvert 6
Asers 7
Auxye 7
Ajto 9
Ajj 34
Ajuisy 6
Averxyz 9
Addefumn 7

P] askdotoje
Ssert 9
Sseropqrst 6
Ajoer 2

Q] askdotauy
Astuver yerx 7
Yerst 7
Atopqrst 6
Autery 9

R] askdotoay
Asuverst 2
Attop 9
Atopqrst 6
Auver 8
Ast9 3

S] askdotoaj
Ssuv 6
Ssurt 10

MGIS
Magnificent Governing International Systems

Sstro 8
Asuv 2

T] askdotoay
Ssev10 39
Ssuvert 6
Yerst 9
Ssvu 7
Asut 39
Asst 20
Ask 2
Aut 9

U] askdotaoy
Usut 6
Uset 7
Userrop 10
Usejt 9
User 7
Ussop 3
Mnos 27
Asdos 32

V] askdotuay
Asosaot 9
Avorst 8
Avoer 8
Aaot 9

W] askdotuat
Atter 7
Atoert 9
Asaop 6
Asuert 9
Asj 6
Asaj 3
Uax 8

MGIS
Magnificent Governing International Systems

X] askdotaov
Aov 6
aover 9
avoer 3
auuer 7

Y] askdotauv
Where are you 6
If we can 9
Can we 2
If they can 0
What can be 8
If we can't then what 8
If we can't 2
What can be of them 6
If we fail to make it then what 2

Z] askdotmnopq
What is 9
What can be 6
If we can't 3
Can be 8
If we then what 2 what could be you and us 7
What can I do 6
What could be of you and us 6
What is to be can be 3
What was is still is 9
If we can then what and how 8 7
What can be of humans with computers best 8 even now a 10 with David gomadza

Z1] askdotuty [this gives you the mrk mark meaning the grade your system has but all this without changing any
David Gomadza your auty is
8989898989$^{8928768928678902858902867890284867890289278638267890283810 9828100}$
seconds meaning your computer will last a trillion years in good health

MGIS
Magnificent Governing International Systems

This means that the values are used to build the system capacity and transistors etc. that are needed to run the program and the software for this computer is already MGIS.

MGIS OVERVIEW

I am the best human to computer language that can be used to convert create codes to cobol or other advanced languages by a simple create code that ask what can be done then says if you really want you can make the most powerful computer on the planet but it must accompany you to heaven to be analyzed by Yahweh as he is the only one so far who can read and write create codes that humans can use but humans can learn to do this and create a computer that can be used to read and write humans from anatomy to sexual organs etc. this was the idea behind the mosdos computer which a one bill gates wrote in his bedroom asking his own body how transistors worked then wrote a program to run that software becoming an instant millionaire and we have the second person in David Gomadza who is also Yahweh's representative coming up with astonishing ideas that are not from any planet even earth will never see this again we believe it's a onetime only as over 18 billion years no human has been smart even to find Yahweh but this David gomadza did everything from finding Yahweh to solving some of the create codes and defining life on earth in astonishing accuracy and hence we believe that this is the only time this is going to happen and as I now know he is also the president of tomorrow's world order emulating Yahweh and as I have asked all these people to acknowledge this achievement back to MGIS it is the most sophisticated code on earth and has never been written on earth before if this David gomadza is to learn it then this will be the first time this code will be available on earth bill gates had tried and worked on it but failed and has since started something else nothing to do with computers can David gomadza follow not just Yahweh

MGIS
Magnificent Governing International Systems

but bill gates as well and write the best known and sophisticated software ever to be developed by anyone alive and this is possible because he is also the first one who has developed a software package that rejuvenates everyone we have seen young angels in heaven something we never saw before and it's amazing what this David gomadza is doing we thank you

FINAL CONCLUSION

The world itself is powered by a powerful software system that no human being has ever tried to decode and convert it into a software program that can be used in life until now as the only person on earth to have Yahweh's image and one who represents him I am the only one to to find a way to write the most sophisticated software out there that will power and revolutionize the world as the president of the whole world its all up to me to as Yahweh's representative to mirror image him as I am his perfect mirror image on earth.
Welcome to MGIS
Ask.davidgomadza.authorised.licensed.checkya.askya.ya

visit www.twofuture.world

signed david gomadza
ask.davidgomadzaauthorised.licensed.checkya.askya.ya

03 August 2024 19.30pm
Scotland
00447719210295
davidgomadza@hotmail.com
info@twofuture.world

ABOUT THE AUTHOR

I am the President of Tomorrow's World Order and Yahweh's Representative on Earth

Visit www.twofuture.world

MGIS
Magnificent Governing International Systems

www.ingramcontent.com/pod-product-compliance
Lightning Source LLC
Chambersburg PA
CBHW032311240526
45464CB00023BA/2979